The Transcontinental Railroad

James P. Burger

The Rosen Publishing Group's
PowerKids Press™
New York

For Joseph Thomas, working on the railroad

Published in 2002 by The Rosen Publishing Group, Inc.
29 East 21st Street, New York, NY 10010

Copyright © 2002 by The Rosen Publishing Group, Inc.

First Edition

Book Design: Emily Muschinske
Project Editor: Kathy Campbell

Photo Credits: title page, pp. 4 (poster), 8, 15 (Chinese workers), 16, 20 (boomtown), 22 © The Granger Collection, New York; p. 4 (wagon train) © Archive Photos; p. 7 (Theodore Judah) © ; pp. 7 (map), 15 (Cornish workers), 19 (Cheyenne), 19 (buffalo) © North Wind Picture Archives; p. 11 (background) © SuperStock; pp. 11 (inset), 12 (inset), 12 (background) Hulton Getty Collection/Archive Photos; p. 20 (gamblers) American Stock/Archive Photos; train icon throughout © Newberry Library, Chicago/SuperStock.

Burger, James P.
The Transcontinental Railroad / James P. Burger.
    p. cm. — (The Library of the westward expansion)
Includes bibliographical references and index.
  ISBN 0-8239-5852-3 (library binding)
1. Railroads—United States—History—19th century—Juvenile literature. 2. Union Pacific Railroad Company—History—Juvenile literature. 3. Central Pacific Railroad Company—History—Juvenile literature, [1. Railroads—West (U.S.)—History. 2. Union Pacific Railroad Company—History. 3. Central Pacific Railroad Company—History.] I. Title.
  TF23 .B85 2002
  385'.0978—dc21
                                                                00–013208

Manufactured in the United States of America

Contents

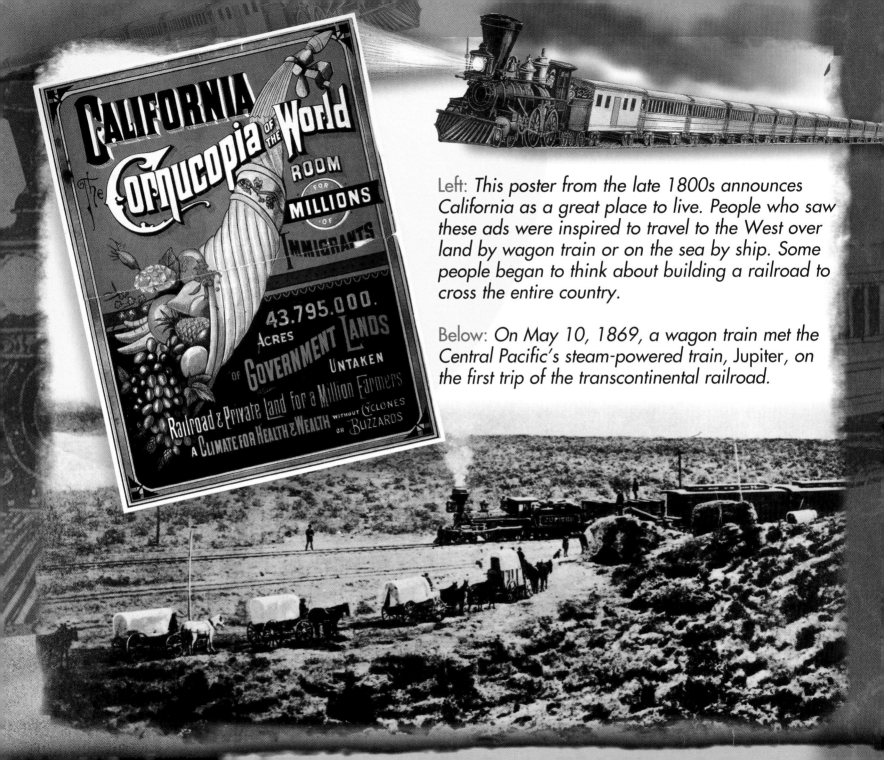

Left: *This poster from the late 1800s announces California as a great place to live. People who saw these ads were inspired to travel to the West over land by wagon train or on the sea by ship. Some people began to think about building a railroad to cross the entire country.*

Below: *On May 10, 1869, a wagon train met the Central Pacific's steam-powered train, Jupiter, on the first trip of the transcontinental railroad.*

Manifest Destiny

During the mid-1800s, many Americans had a common goal, which they called Manifest Destiny. Most Americans lived in the states and **territories** between the Atlantic Ocean and the Mississippi River. Manifest Destiny meant that the United States had the right and duty to expand beyond the Mississippi River, all the way to the Pacific Ocean. Explorers had mapped this western land during the early 1800s, so the U.S. government already knew what a lot of it looked like. The government decided to sell the rich land in the wilderness to Americans who wanted to farm it.

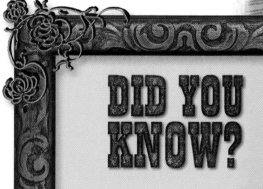

DID YOU KNOW?

During the 1840s, hundreds of thousands of people loaded covered wagons with supplies and possessions and headed to Oregon to farm and to escape the East's overcrowded cities.

Crazy Judah and the Big Four

Many railroads already crisscrossed the East. Theodore Judah, a successful railroad **engineer** in the East, dreamed of building a **transcontinental** railroad. He told many people about his plan. Most thought that such a railroad would be too long and hard to build. They thought only someone crazy could think up such an idea, so they **nicknamed** him Crazy Judah. Judah and his wife moved to California in 1854. There Judah built the state's first railroad in less than a year. He was still planning a transcontinental railroad when he met businessmen Leland Stanford, Charles Crocker, Mark Hopkins, and Collis Huntington in 1861. These men believed that people would pay to ride such a railroad, and they wanted to own it. The four rich businessmen created the Central Pacific Railroad Company in April 1861, and called themselves the Big Four.

Above: *This map shows all the transcontinental railroad routes that were created after the Central Pacific Railroad joined its tracks with the tracks of the Union Pacific Railroad in 1869.*

Right: *Theodore Judah got four businessmen to give him money to start building the transcontinental railroad. Together they formed the Central Pacific Railroad Company.*

PROMONTORY SUMMIT

The Pacific Railroad Act

In April 1861, the American Civil War broke out between the North and the South. **Politicians** from 11 southern states left Washington, D.C., to form the **Confederate States of America**. Politicians from the North stayed in Washington. They believed that building a railroad to the West could help the **Union** army surround the South and win the Civil War. On July 1, 1862, President Abraham Lincoln signed the Pacific Railroad Act to fund and build a transcontinental railroad. The U.S. government wanted companies to **compete** with each other to make the best railroad possible.

This famous photograph by A. J. Russell shows the celebration of the workers and engineers on May 10, 1869, at Promontory Summit, Utah. A worker drove in the last spike here, joining the eastern and western tracks of the transcontinental railroad.

DID YOU KNOW?

The Central Pacific Railroad Company planned to build the western half of the railroad, beginning at Sacramento, California. The Union Pacific Railroad Company planned to build from the East, starting at Council Bluffs, Iowa. They wanted to race to see who could build the most track.

9

Chinese Laborers

The Central Pacific began building its part of the railroad on January 8, 1863, but the company had a hard time finding workers. Many men who were hired worked only until they reached Nevada. Then they left, hoping to strike it rich in the Nevada silver mines that had been found in 1859.

Many Chinese **immigrants** had come to California to search for gold during the gold rush of the 1850s. Charles Crocker hired Chinese laborers to build the railroad through the mountain range of the Sierra Nevada, on the border of California and Nevada. The rest of the Big Four doubted that Chinese workers could build such a railroad because many were physically small. Crocker thought that, because they had built the Great Wall of China, the Chinese surely could build a railroad through the mountains.

Inset: *Central Pacific crews like this one included people from China.* Bottom: *These Chinese workers are building part of the railroad in Sacramento, California. Central Pacific bosses watched in wonder as Chinese laborers worked quickly and steadily without complaining.*

Top: *This Union Pacific work crew takes a break by supply wagons.*

Bottom: *Workers laying tracks along the side of a mountain use a steam shovel to lift rocks after blasting.*

The Union Pacific's Slow Start

The Union Pacific had an easier job than the Central Pacific. The Union Pacific could quickly lay track across the flat prairies of today's **Midwest**. It did face problems, though. It lacked money. The government would give money to the Union Pacific, but only after it had laid long stretches of track. It also lacked workers. The Civil War, which was being fought at this time, took most men to the battlefields. Thomas Durant, a smart businessman who headed the Union Pacific, asked some powerful friends to help him raise money. Durant then hired immigrants to work for the railroad, and the Union Pacific was almost ready to begin construction.

DID YOU KNOW?

Thomas "Doc" Durant hired immigrants to work on the Union Pacific Railroad. Many of these immigrants were Irish and came to the United States to escape a famine in Ireland during the mid-1800s. A famine is a shortage of food that causes people to starve.

Crossing the Sierra Nevada

The Central Pacific's workers had to move tons of rocks and trees to clear a path through the mountain range of the Sierra Nevada. The tops of the mountains were too steep to build the railroad across, so the workers cut tunnels through them. That was very dangerous, slow work. The workers used **nitroglycerin** to blast the rock. Sometimes these workers were hurt badly by large explosions.

In other places, **locomotives** had to go around mountains. To cut **ledges** for tracks that were high up, Chinese laborers wove baskets big enough to hold a man. Laborers would climb into these baskets and be lowered alongside the steep rock to drill holes into the rock face. After placing nitroglycerin inside the holes, the laborers were quickly **hoisted** back up. Then the rock exploded, leaving a ledge for the trains to run along.

Top: *Chinese workers use nitroglycerin to blow up a mountainside. Often the Chinese could tunnel faster than the experienced Cornish.*

Left: *To cut through the mountains, the Central Pacific hired Cornish workers, who had become famous for their drilling skills in Nevada's silver mines.*

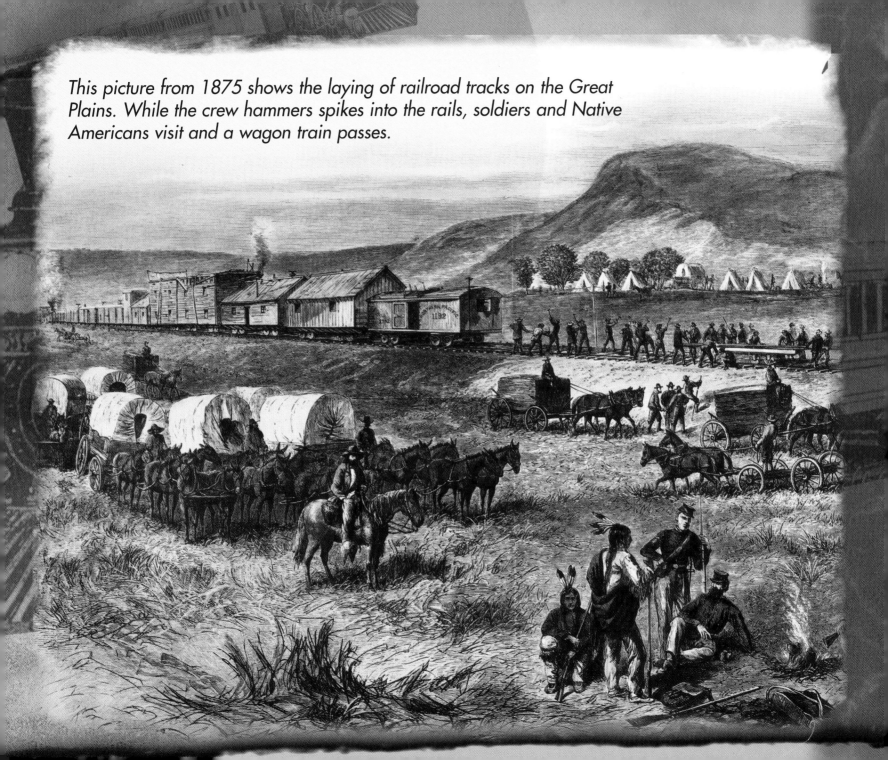

This picture from 1875 shows the laying of railroad tracks on the Great Plains. While the crew hammers spikes into the rails, soldiers and Native Americans visit and a wagon train passes.

Where to Begin?

Many cities in today's Midwest wanted the Union Pacific Railroad to begin in or near their cities. Members of the Union Pacific Railroad Company had their own ideas about the starting place for their tracks. President Lincoln finally decided that the tracks should start in Council Bluffs, Iowa.

On December 2, 1863, the Union Pacific **broke ground**, but not where Lincoln had wanted. Starting in Council Bluffs meant the company would first need to build a long, expensive bridge over the Missouri River. The company paid no attention to Lincoln's directions and started on the western side of the river, in Omaha, Nebraska.

DID YOU KNOW?

While the Central Pacific Railroad Company was still struggling with its route through the Sierra Nevada, the Union Pacific hurried to build as much of its part of the railroad as possible. When they joined their tracks, the transcontinental railroad was about 1,775 miles (2,857 km) long.

Native Americans

As the Union Pacific Railroad bosses and their work crews raced to lay track across the prairies, they met Native Americans. Native Americans had never seen a railroad before, and they did not like it. Buffalo, which the Native Americans hunted for food, ran away from the railroad and became harder for the Native Americans to hunt. Americans settling along the railroad's route sometimes built ranches with fences, so the buffalo could not cross that part of the land. Americans made a sport of killing many buffalo, which also affected the Native Americans' lifestyle.

The farther the railroad **progressed**, the angrier Native Americans became. There were some violent battles between the Native Americans and the railroad workers. Many workers were experienced soldiers. Often they won their battles against the Native Americans and quickly returned to laying the tracks.

Top: *This picture shows the Cheyenne attacking a Union Pacific Railroad crew in 1867.*

Bottom: *In the 1870s, white hunters shot buffalo for sport from "iron horses," as locomotives were called. Buffalo were sacred animals to Native Americans.*

Left: This photograph shows what a common boomtown looked like. Boomtowns were also called shantytowns because the rough buildings, or shanties, were put up quickly.

Bottom: These men gamble in a California boomtown in 1900. Gambling halls and bars gave workers places to spend their wages, which amounted to about $35 each month.

Boomtowns

Towns were built alongside the Union Pacific as the railroad progressed westward. Laborers relaxed in these towns, known as boomtowns, when they weren't working. As the Union Pacific moved west across the land, the towns followed. Some towns were even taken apart, loaded onto freight cars, and carried along the growing route! These towns were rough places surrounded by wilderness. People gambled, drank, and fought with each other. Often fights ended in shootings. Other times, workers drank so much alcohol that they could not work. In 1866, the Union Pacific hired two brothers, Jack and Dan Casement, to help keep the workers in line.

DID YOU KNOW?

The tough Casement brothers quickly ended any type of trouble the railroad workers started. The Casements were so strict that many of the wild towns disappeared. Their help made construction of the railroad possible.

East Meets West

The Central Pacific reached the eastern side of the Sierra Nevada after almost six years of work. Then, racing across flat desert, the work crews often laid 1 mile (1.6 km) of eastward track per day. The Union Pacific crews also worked quickly. The Union Pacific had laid 1,085 miles (1,746 km) of track from Omaha westward to Promontory Summit, Utah. The Central Pacific had laid 690 miles (1,110.5 km) of track from Sacramento eastward to Promontory Summit. Around 12:00 P.M., on May 10, 1869, a worker hammered the last spike, a golden spike, into the railroad. The transcontinental railroad finally connected the East with the West. Soon thousands of people boarded trains to cross the country.

This special golden spike joined the Central Pacific and Union Pacific tracks of the transcontinental railroad on May 10, 1869. Its inscription reads "The Pacific Railroad ground broken January 8th 1863 and completed May 8th 1869."

Glossary

broke ground (BROHK GROWND) Began digging at the start of a construction project.

compete (kum-PEET) Trying hard to win something.

Confederate States of America (kun-FEH-duh-ret STAYTZ UV uh-MER-ih-kuh) A group of 11 southern states that declared themselves separate from the United States in 1860–61.

engineer (en-jih-NEER) A person who is an expert at planning and building engines, machines, roads, bridges, and canals.

hoisted (HOYST-ed) Lifted or pulled up.

immigrants (IH-muh-grints) People who have moved to a new country from another country.

ledges (LEH-jez) Narrow rock shelves along the edges of cliffs.

locomotives (loh-kuh-MOH-tivz) The first train cars that pull the rest of the cars.

Midwest (mid-WEST) The Middle West, a region in the north-central United States.

nicknamed (NIK-naymd) To have been given a funny and interesting name that is used instead of a person's or thing's real name.

nitroglycerin (ny-troh-GLIHS-rin) A very explosive substance.

politicians (pah-lih-TIH-shins) People who hold or run for a public office.

progressed (pruh-GREHSD) Got further.

territories (TEHR-uh-tor-eez) Lands that are controlled by a person or group of people.

transcontinental (tranz-kon-tin-EN-tul) Going across a continent.

Union (YOON-yun) The northern states during the Civil War.

Index

Web Sites

To learn more about the transcontinental railroad, check out these Web sites:

http://cprr.org/Museum/index.html
www.csrmf.org